APHIDS IN THE ROSE

poems by

Joan Baranow

Finishing Line Press
Georgetown, Kentucky

APHIDS IN THE ROSE

With gratitude to everyone who took care of me during my treatments and for those who share the cancer journey

Copyright © 2023 by Joan Baranow
ISBN 979-8-88838-181-6 First Edition
All rights reserved under International and Pan-American Copyright Conventions. No part of this book may be reproduced in any manner whatsoever without written permission from the publisher, except in the case of brief quotations embodied in critical articles and reviews.

ACKNOWLEDGMENTS

The author thanks the editors of the journals in which the following poems appeared:

The Art of Medicine in Metaphor: "Lumpectomy"
Chest Journal: "Consultation Before Surgery"
Community of Writers 50th Anniversary Anthology: "Follow-up Appointment"
The Healing Muse: "Catch and Release"
JAMA: "Side Effects"
Medmic—Conversations, Culture & Creativity from the Health Care Community: "Routine Mammogram"
Poetics for the More Than Human World: "Drought"
Tell Me Again—Poetry and Prose from The Healing Art of Writing: "Checking Margins"
The Western Journal of Medicine: "Aphids in the Rose"

Publisher: Leah Huete de Maines
Editor: Christen Kincaid
Cover Art: Jeffrey Ventrella
Author Photo: David Watts
Cover Design: Elizabeth Maines McCleavy

Order online: www.finishinglinepress.com
also available on amazon.com

Author inquiries and mail orders:
Finishing Line Press
PO Box 1626
Georgetown, Kentucky 40324
USA

Table of Contents

Consultation before Surgery ... 1

Aphids in the Rose ... 2

Malignancy ... 3

Infection ... 4

Signals ... 5

Follow-up Appointment ... 6

Catch and Release ... 7

Red ... 8

Letting Go ... 9

Coastal Route ... 10

Inserting the IV ... 11

Checking Margins ... 12

On the Playground ... 13

God Confesses ... 15

Drought ... 16

Side Effects ... 17

Leaning Against a Tree ... 18

A Brief Reprieve ... 19

At the Cancer Center ... 20

Gratitude ... 21

Snowy Tree Cricket ... 22

Lumpectomy ... 23

Wonderland ... 24

Routine Mammogram ... 25

You think it will never happen to you,
What happens every day to other women.

    —Alicia Ostriker, "The Bridge" from *The Mastectomy Poems*

all night it is the one breast
comforting the other

    —Lucille Clifton, "lumpectomy eve"

Consultation before Surgery

With her finger touching the pink
and purple diagram, the doc explains
dye will flow through milk ducts
to the Sentinel Lymph Nodes,
making tracer stains
where the scalpel must go.
She doesn't need to say that cells
are pawns of nature's lunatic changes,
that no one's guilty,
nor that years nuzzling those
little packages
wrapped in baby blankets
failed to protect the breast.
Something in you opened,
your cup runneth over
and emptied.
We're here now, she says,
whatever the past was.
Get dressed. Don't fret.
And so,
you comb through her brisk words
and find she's right, death backs off,
while inside, seething, voracious
cells keep eating estrogen,
growing fat
from your bruised, but
still intact, breast.

Aphids in the Rose

Trying with a damp Q-tip
to swipe aphids off the rosebush,
I wonder what concussion occurred
inside my body, which cell it was
that woke up one morning with its RNA
gone nuts, a crazed terrorist
who tortures himself.
The doctor confirmed earlier reports
of inexplicable madness, my cells
giving in to strange demands:
shoes on backwards, hands waving out of ears,
whole neighborhoods of nuclei
dancing maniacally.
I had seen pictures of cells
undergoing their dignified divisions—
rows of identical platoons
splitting their heads in half—
and then for no apparent reason,
the sergeant shouts the right words
in the wrong order, her error
rippling through ranks, undeciphered.
Meanwhile, citizens are fleeing the cities
with wounds that can kill them.
The doctor says my best hope is to
burn the thing down below ground level,
the deeper the better.
She's one of those who knows
the good effects of death.
I'm still poking at these flimsy aphids,
arguing against myself,
wincing at each surrender.

Malignancy

Somewhat the same
as when swelling with milk—
weighty, warm, with weird

prickles, only there's no miraculous
milk slipping through ducts,
no colostrum

beading the porous nipples, no—
it's a sensation
the surgeons can't explain,

mimicking the maternal—
a host of hungry
cells feeding off cells.

Infection

The hibiscus has a brown rash
no expert can explain.
It's been like this for weeks.
Likewise the rose with its rust.
We do what we can with what we've got,
which isn't much.
A spray might dissolve the stain.
Pruning might let new leaves
unfurl from the meristems.
We can hope.
We tend to the lives we let in,
knowing little about their care.
We, as in I, the amateur.

Signals

The maples on our hill
struggle to leaf out
this third year of drought.
It seems the trees survive
on mist alone
falling over the ridge,
beyond which the ocean
warms and warms,
tossing heaps of jellyfish
onto the beach.

This morning the town
hums its usual tune
of SUVs—nearby, a bird keeps
launching its insistent call
without response.
A truck with two ladders
strapped like lifeboats
crawls up the street.

Even a distant siren
doesn't perturb the April air.
At the center of shock
is perfect stillness,
from which waves of pain
can crush anything
without sound.

Follow-up Appointment

You'd think that inside the open incision
the tumor would declare itself
as obvious, a hard pit
darkish and persistent,
unwilling to let the flesh go,
but the surgeon explains that cancer
looks like healthy tissue,
that's why the marker with its metal hook
gets pushed in,
why she must excise widely
to keep the margins clean.
Similar, I suppose, to skirting
around a volatile dog
or how, just this afternoon, I kept
a good distance between me and the guy
dancing outside the gas station,
who asked, "How're you doing, Sweetheart?"
and I said, "Fine, thanks,"
and felt, actually, a little happy
even as I glanced quickly away,
my body still visibly female,
all of me as yet intact,
even my blonde-dyed hair.

Catch and Release

You're allowed to breathe in intervals.
Women you'll never see again
take an interest in your breast.

They have careful hands. They understand
where to aim the dart.

The dart snags red minnows of tissue.

They hook your tumor,
pay out string through a hole
punched in a paper cup.

The surgeon a fisher of women,
yourself a river
invaded by unlikely species—

Bighead carp below the Ohio
shoving aside the benign bass.

She traces her line,
splits the surface, scoops
with a sharp net.

You lie stilled in your flow, caught briefly,
before you're sewn up and let go.

Red

Paper hearts cut with safety scissors.
Jack knife. Chipped nail polish.
Crescent of kiss on the cup.

Brash Snow Plant
in a field of needles. Prairie Fire.
The plaid shirt of the wildflower expert.

Alizarin crimson dabbed on the palette.
She squints to see the skin's flush.
Drapery. Genital petals.

Strips snagged from the breast
stained for the diagnosis.
The pathologist's bitten lip.

A winter dawn.
The last flash before the earth
turns away.

Letting Go

The massive redwood gives up,
glides to the side, silent,

expelling its breath—
that's what I want,

to topple freely,
my trunk splintering

into long, jagged spears,
my roots as useless

as high heels snapped off.
That's it—

the full weight of gravity
pulling

with its fiery core,
whose hold never slips,

whose fist releases
such glossy, improbable leaves.

Coastal Route

Rain sheens the windshield,
the off road ocean crushes
scattered granite,
shoulders surf shoreward.

It's that side of earth
hard to hear from here
inside my metal.
Not a tin coffin but could be

so keep peeks minimal.
The sky gushes. Must be flowers
hold their breath. I would too
if stripped out there, nothing but

petals between me and whatever.
Where do the deer go?
Such thin fur I could worry and do.
No dry hollow to duck into,

no brush not drenched. Somewhere
all the wet animals unaccountable.
Slicked feathers. Upturned worms.
A gull just standing there.

Inserting the IV

She came in carrying the saline lock,
upbeat, her hair like blanched wheat
around her healthy face.
I turned away, closed my eyes,
felt the needle test my vein,
the easy one that won't resist.

"I'm messy," she said, "but
really good at this."

Blood rolled down my arm,
past my wrist, all the way
to fingertips, and kept running,
a damaged faucet that won't shut off.

Checking Margins

She went in twice to be sure
and found nothing more
like going back to check a cold stove.
Gas is invisible to the casual eye,
the same as breast cancer,
until cells start elbowing each other,
spilling drinks, scattering crumbs
across the mammography floor.
By then the only recourse is eviction,
for which preparation must be made,
poisons procured. Ever after
the world is weirdly foreshortened,
like that picture of the far
star that blew 10 billion years ago,
whose light is just now
reaching this room.

On the Playground

>   *for T—*

He's here to pick up his kids and looking good,
his hair still intact, sporting
a week's growth of grey, attractive beard.
He's feeling okay so far, after two rounds of chemo
with eight to go.

In the old days the cure would kill you
and nothing much has changed
when it comes to a rare non-Hodgkin's
large T-cell B-cell lymphoma.
He says he'll be in the ICU for thirty days
for a bone marrow transplant,
and I can tell the future
for him is as vague as Alaska.
His wife whispers how
he screamed when the needle
broke through bone on the biopsy table.
He's got three boys under the age of ten.

*

Sometimes you catch a pickax on your tongue.
Sometimes you're made to carry your own heart.

Sometimes the only air you can breathe
has been burnt several times over.

Sometimes God passes through your skin
and alters a piece of DNA
just to see you writhe.

Sometimes screams fly from the throat
as if they'd been crouching there,

a crush of ravens
scissoring each other with their wings.

Sometimes you recover and start over,
weak and bald as a baby.

Sometimes you don't.

*

I tell my friend we're here to help
and he says it's going to be a long haul,
a euphemism for hell.
He's off now with his wife and kids,
making plans for a weekend bike ride.

I touch the missing tissue
that had once rounded my breast
the way believers rub a coin for good luck.

God Confesses

DNA spun its way out of me, twisting
like a yo-yo
spooling around-the-world

and then wind gushed
from my orifices.

I was outside
and inside at once,
roots crawling through my belly,
clouds in my chest.
No one had warned me
about motion sickness,
no one there to hold me
as I vomited gobs of swamp.

He's perfect, they say,
in prayers and hosannas.
I keep looking in glassy lakes,
searching my eyes for a flaw.

If only they'd test my genetic sequence,
get my fingerprints,
subject me to questioning
under the hot bulb,
I'd confess without a fuss.

I had no one to guide me.
I was making it up as I went along.
Have mercy.

Drought

These hills are green again
with grasses fine and fleeting—
like lanugo, it won't last.

Each year rain recedes,
the oceans churn their plastics.
Almond trees and cattle feed
drink the ground dry.

On this parched lip of land,
we watch the signs,
pocket profits, project
the desiccations of earth.

When the water's gone,
when the hills are stripped
of deer and birdsong,
we will wander across
the cracked valley
on unbalanced accounts,

east from San Joaquin,
towards Reno.

Side Effects

You wake up one morning and find
you're encased in someone else's skin.
So this is what the much-touted
alien invasion was all about.
They should have at least given you
a certificate, or your favorite hyacinth.
Instead, they crawled in
through every tight orifice
to play badminton across your chest.
They've fashioned ingenious boats
from bone chips and are now
angling through your aortic valve,
crowding the rail to get a glimpse
of your pulsing bloody heart,
your vast, mitochondrial operations.
But soon after the bon voyage,
the hulls scrape bottom, breach
capillary walls,
and it's the Titanic all over again,
blue, horror-struck, gasping—who knew
aliens need to breathe like we do?
By now you're writhing in bed,
reading up on Anastrozole and its many
unpleasant effects.
You wonder if your affairs are in order,
if those tiny scientists will
get back to their flagship in time.

Leaning Against a Tree

I press the rough pelt,
my ear to the actual bark.

Is it my mother's death? My marriage?
My malignant breast? Tell me.

Wind shushes the leaves,
preparing to speak.

I am holding my breath.
The rocks are waiting.

The trees are trying to remember.

A Brief Reprieve

Here beside the blue bay
the steady clank of a pile driver

roughs up the calm
like a wind-up toy stuck on.

Yet the wind is warm, the laurels
dip and rise as they do,

the water true enough to imagine
diving in,

breaking the sun into rings.
How strange, to be young again,

to slip off my dress
and wade out into the waiting depths,

adrift, like a lopsided starfish
licked by the current … but now

the clock insists on my presence.
And the ditch-digger resumes its roar.

At the Cancer Center

*You can keep your shoes on,
don't you move, we'll move you.*

I'm in my gown, lying down,
arms overhead, positioned
according to the angles
the terse technician
stenciled to my chest.

Large, heavy, ponderous,
the accelerator rises up
like a charcoal moon
that orbits over me,
exhaling photons,
before it sinks back down
where I can't see.

A friend asks,
"How's the radiation going?"
and I think of these
three motionless minutes
where all I need do
is lie down and be still—
I even get to breathe.

Gratitude

> *...health is whatever works*
> *and for as long.*
>   — John Stone, "He Makes a House Call"

I'm working on my sense of gratitude.
I admit I have less than my proper share of it.

To practice, I exclaim over flowers
that grow from roadside rubble.

I remind myself that my children
have skirted past
any number of car accidents.

The fact that the earth keeps spinning
deserves my astonishment.

I have clean water from a tap,
a full tin of tea.

When I come home,
I hear the laugh of a friend, waiting for me.

Snowy Tree Cricket

Tucked in pink lantana,
your song starts as the sky
fills with lit confetti.

You scrape your legs
like the way I rub my feet
together in bed, with possibly
the same pleasure.

I've seen you a few times
all wings and angles.
It's no use asking what
hand or eye made your lullaby.

These days I'm listening
for your pitch, 3 kHz
pulsing trills—
your shrill, reliable opera.

Lumpectomy

The moon is a little dented tonight
on the right side
where an arm would be
pressing,
and that's natural
to the moon
as well as certain situations—
a word gets slivered off,
a cup chips its lip—
and accidents,
like standing up into
a harder substance
than your head.
Soon, though, the moon
regains her whole,
there's repair
to blood and hair
where force
asserted its fact,
and bone builds
within its cracks
denser deposits.
Every form exhibits
the seams of what was
torn or taken or lost.
Lovely
the life left
with its stitches.
Even this night
tucked between granite peaks
receives from a surface
slightly skewed
a bruised
yet no less emphatic
radiance.

Wonderland

for Judy

Snow on the spruce boughs,
snow on the car roof
hard to shove off
the unreachable middle,
which is fine because
what would life be
without the untasted possibility
of tomorrow's dessert,
a two-foot mound of iced
cake, all spirals and sugar pearls,
as daring as pyramids
or a flight to the moon,
those guys suited up
with their own oxygen,
jumping in slow-mo like baby kangaroos.

Friend, we knew it would be beautiful,
tree after tree loaded with snow,
heartsap slowed to a coma,
the trail lost in hip-deep drifts.
If you're lucky, you'll find
a scrap of bear fur,
sticks of kindling,
a place to build your igloo
outside the neighbor's view.
This wind tips a branch,
lets fall a cups-worth of snow.
You lift its brilliance to your lips
and hear the improbable
calls of wintering
chickadees.

Routine Mammogram

> *But even the very hairs of your head are all numbered.*
> *Fear not therefore…*
> *Luke 12:7 King James Bible*

The young technician waves me in.
The light is dim, the glass plate cold
against my breast
where she spreads it, practiced

at positioning the skin's puckered folds
for the craniocaudal view—
Hold your breath, relax . . . step back
And then the mediolateral
view, and then the other breast
with its marker showing
where the surgeon cut my cancer out.

I'm grateful for this,
for the doctor saying,
Your tumor's small,
you've got a month of radiation,
then Tamoxifen.
You'll look back on this
as just a radar blip.

It's true. I look back each year
as x-rays pass through
my tissue, grateful
for the science that saved me,
the luck that spared me.

I write this in November 2021,
while half the country
takes chances with contagion.
Covid or cancer—we can't predict
whose damaged proteins
can't be cured.

But today an early rain falls,
our season's fires are out.
I slip my bra back on, button up.
Most of me unscathed,
I leave the clinic in my raincoat
and count the number of my days.

Joan Baranow is the author of six poetry collections. Her book, *Reading Szymborska in a Time of Plague*, won the 2021 Brick Road Press contest. Her poems have appeared in *The Gettysburg Review, The Paris Review, Blackbird, Poetry East, JAMA,* and elsewhere. A fellow of the Virginia Center for the Creative Arts and member of the Community of Writers, she founded and teaches in the Low-Residency MFA program in Creative Writing at Dominican University of CA. With her husband David Watts she produced the PBS documentary *Healing Words: Poetry & Medicine*. Her feature-length documentary, *The Time We Have*, presents an intimate portrait of a teenager facing terminal illness.

www.ingramcontent.com/pod-product-compliance
Lightning Source LLC
Chambersburg PA
CBHW022126090426
42743CB00008B/1024